a Plague of FROGS

Cut-Out, Fold and Paste, Paper Model Construction Book for Passover
by

Yaakov Kirschen

ISBN: 9657619092
ISBN-978-965-7619-09-4:

This is a book of paper models of frogs for you to cut out and put together. Use it as a fun activity for the whole family. Children and adults can enjoy it together. Cut, fold, bend and glue the frogs to display on your Passover Seder table or use them as name place settings. The book makes a lovely gift. Educational and fun. Each of the twenty models in this book accurately shows the colors and patterns of different species of frogs from around the world.

Note: To build these models all you'll need is a pair of scissors and a glue stick or white paste glue. Popping up the frog eyes requires use of a razor knife, so it's optional.

The Plague of Frogs

I hope that the frog models in this book will find their places on festive Passover Seder tables everywhere. I've chosen to present twenty frogs out of the hundreds of real world colorful varieties.

You might use these frogs to decorate your Seder table with a cute plague of frogs, or write your guests' names on them to use as place cards, or use them as Sukkah decorations, or offer them to kids as neat holiday-appropriate gifts.

Passover celebrates the freeing of the Israelites from slavery in Egypt. The Bible and the Passover Haggadah describe ten great plagues that struck Egypt and finally convinced Pharaoh to "let our people go".

The second of those ten plagues was a plague of frogs. Most people think that frogs are green, but frogs are found in an amazing number of colors; red, green, blue, purple, yellow, orange, and more. Some have smooth skin, some bumpy, some are one solid color, others have crazy patterns of contrasting colors.

Some frog varieties live in wet, lush rainforests, and others in dry parched deserts, some frogs live up in trees, some live down on the ground. Frogs live almost everywhere on our planet.

Whenever I think of the plague of frogs, of this magical moment in our history, I imagine the land of Egypt being overrun with hundreds of different types of frogs. In my mind I picture frogs from all over the world, pouring into Pharaoh's kingdom in huge colorful, swarming crowds. It was this vision that gave birth to this book and to its selection of frogs from around the world.

Have fun, Enjoy!
Yaakov Kirschen

Instructions

1. Putting your frogs together is really easy. But you'll need to take note of where the "bend here" line between the "nose" and the "front" panels is.

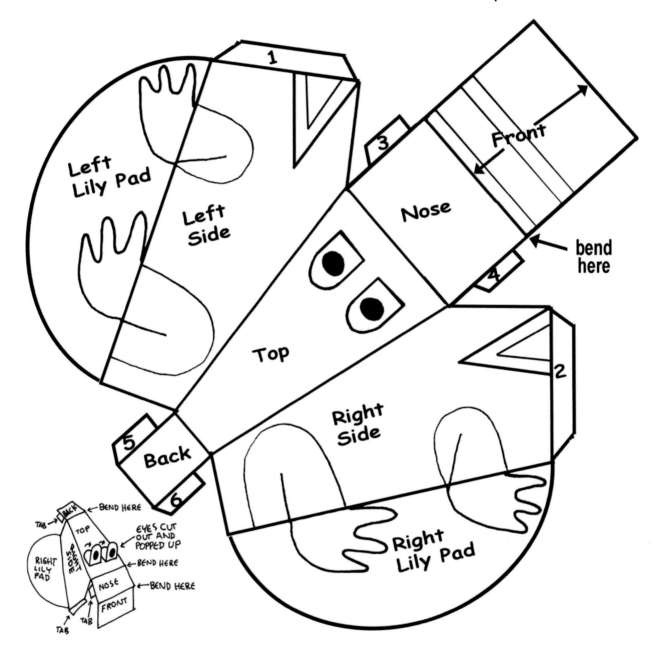

2. Begin by cutting out the frog pattern in one piece, This is easier if you first remove the whole page from the book by cutting along the dotted line to the left of each model.

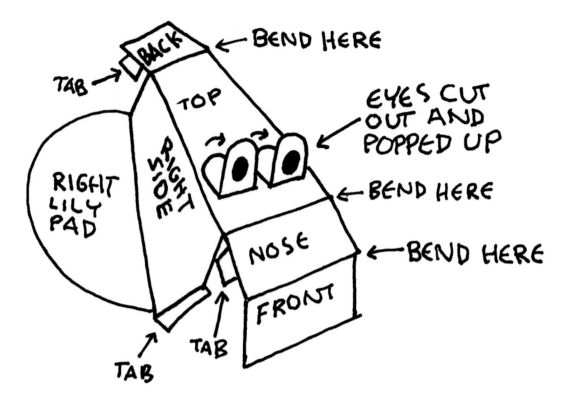

3. Eyes: Popping up the eyes is optional. It's your choice. But it's a choice for adults only because it requires using a razor knife to slice around the U-shape of each eye and then popping them **up** (using the straight line as a hinge). Definitely not for kids to attempt!

4. Whether or not you've popped the eyes, the next step is to bend the "Left Side" and "Right Side" panels **down.**

5. Bend the two half circle Lily pad panels **up**, and bend the "Back" and "Nose" panels **down**.

6. Bend the "Front" panel **down** along the "bend here" line between the "nose" and the "front" panels as shown on the opposite page.

7. Bend each of the six tabs **down** and spread glue on them. (use either white library paste or a UHU glue stick).

8. Glue Tabs 3 and 4 to the "Nose" panel.

9. Glue Tabs 1 and 2 to the "Front" panel.

10. Glue Tabs 5 and 6 to the "Back" panel.

11. If your finished frog model is lumpy congratulations. Real frogs are lumpy too!!

The Paper Models

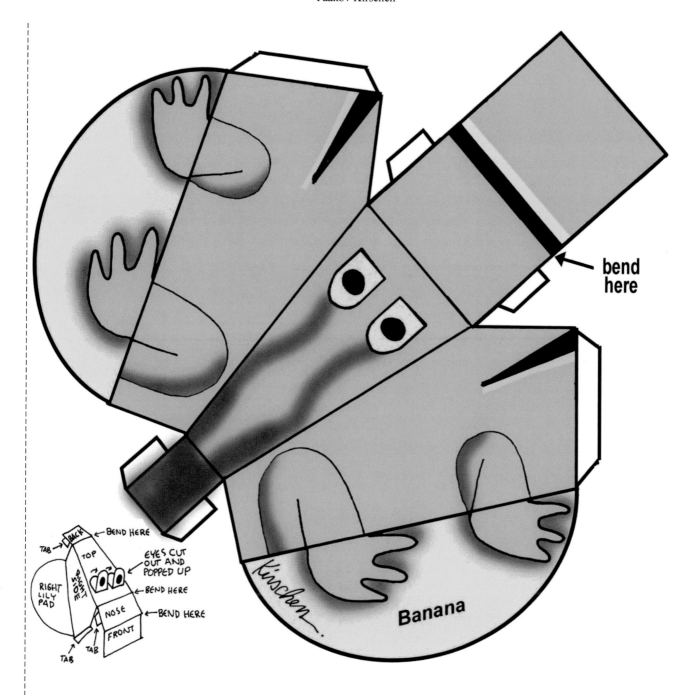

Banana Frog

Banana Frogs are native to South Africa.

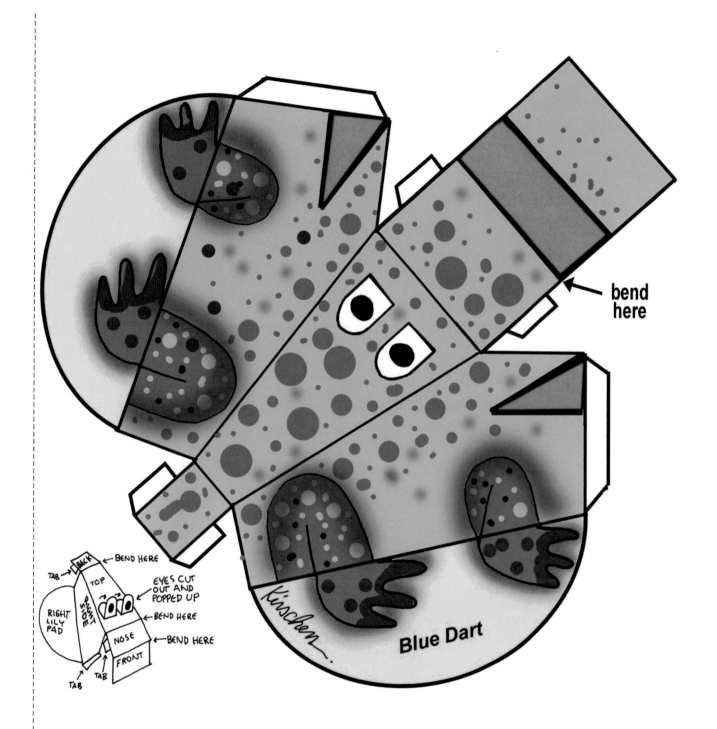

The cut-out model includes labels: bend here, BEND HERE, TAB, BACK, TOP, RIGHT SIDE, EYES CUT OUT AND POPPED UP, BEND HERE, RIGHT LILY PAD, NOSE, BEND HERE, FRONT, TAB, TAB, Kirschen, Blue Dart

Blue Dart Frog

Poison Dart Frogs live in the rainforests of Central and South America.

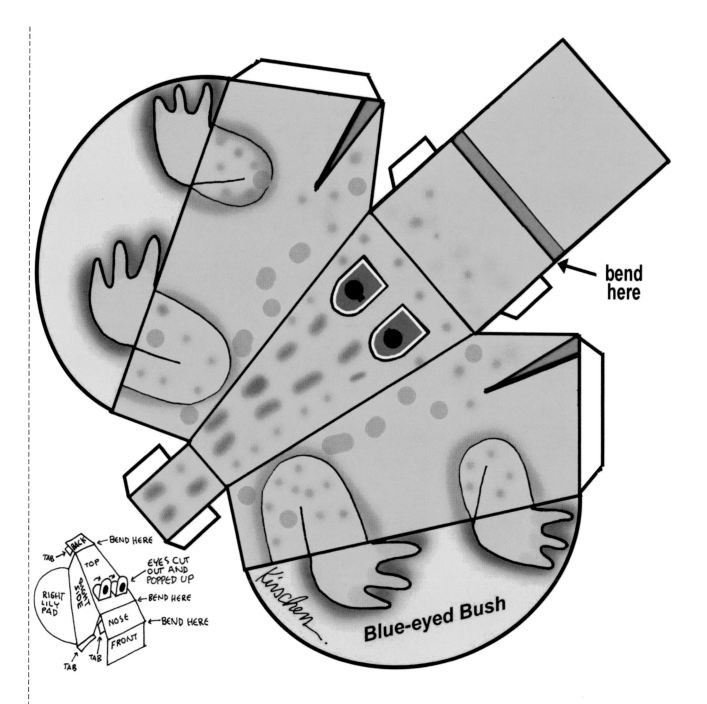

Blue-eyed Bush

Blue-eyed Bush Frog

The Blue-eyed Bush Frog is plentiful in the Indian state of Karnataka (in the southwest of the country).

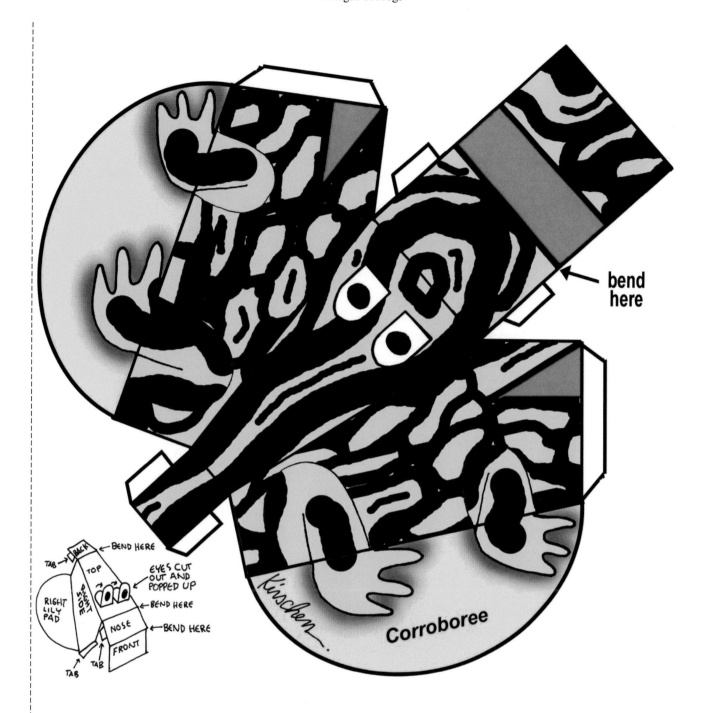

Corroboree

Corroboree Frog

This small, vividly-colored and rare species has only been found in Australia's Kosciuszko National Park (in the south-east of New South Wales).

Yaakov Kirschen

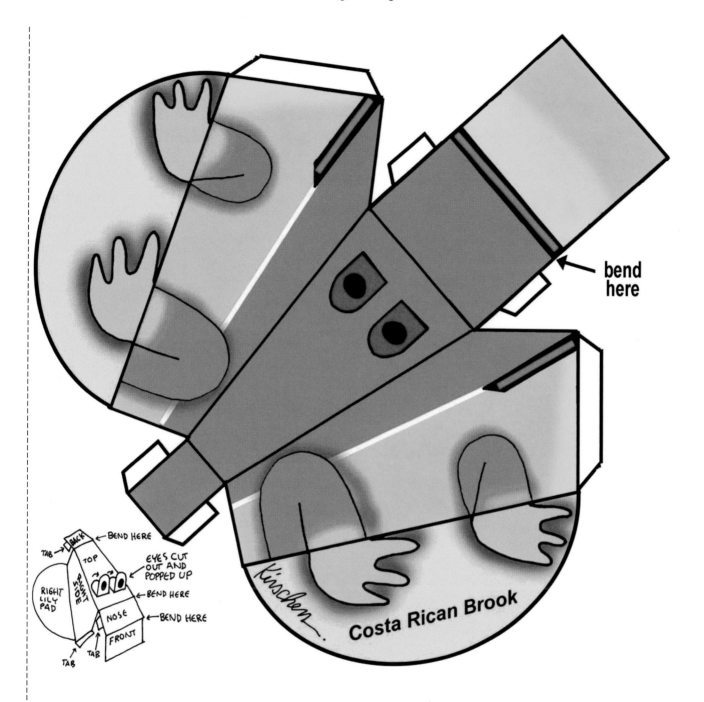

bend
here

BEND HERE
TAB
BACK
TOP
EYES CUT
OUT AND
POPPED UP
RIGHT
LILY
PAD
RIGHT
SIDE
BEND HERE
NOSE
BEND HERE
FRONT
TAB
TAB

Kinschen

Costa Rican Brook

Costa Rican Brook Frog

Found in Costa Rica and western Panama.

Yaakov Kirschen

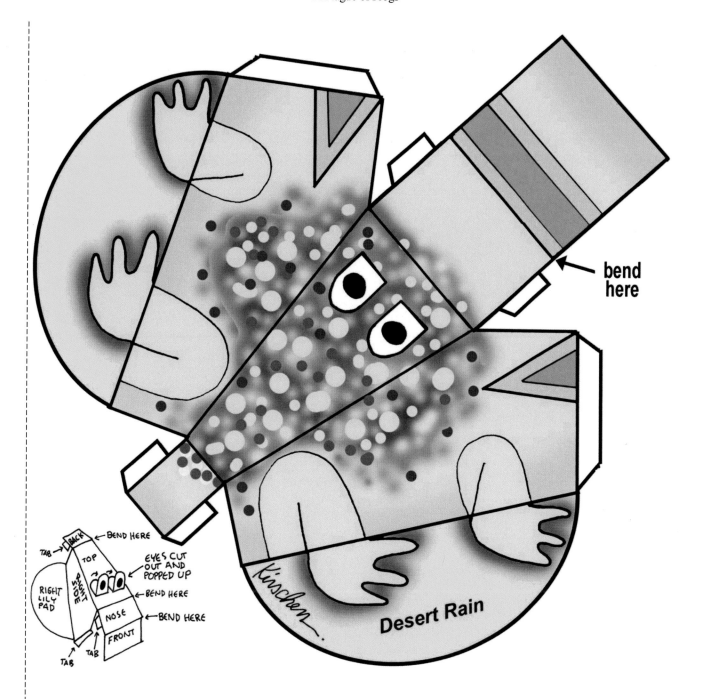

bend
here

BEND HERE
TAB
BACK
TOP
RIGHT
LILY
PAD
RIGHT
SIDE
EYES CUT
OUT AND
POPPED UP
BEND HERE
NOSE
BEND HERE
FRONT
TAB
TAB

Kirschen

Desert Rain

Desert Rain Frog

Desert Rain Frogs are native to Namibia and South Africa.
Their natural habitat is the narrow strip of sandy shores
between the sea and the sand dunes.

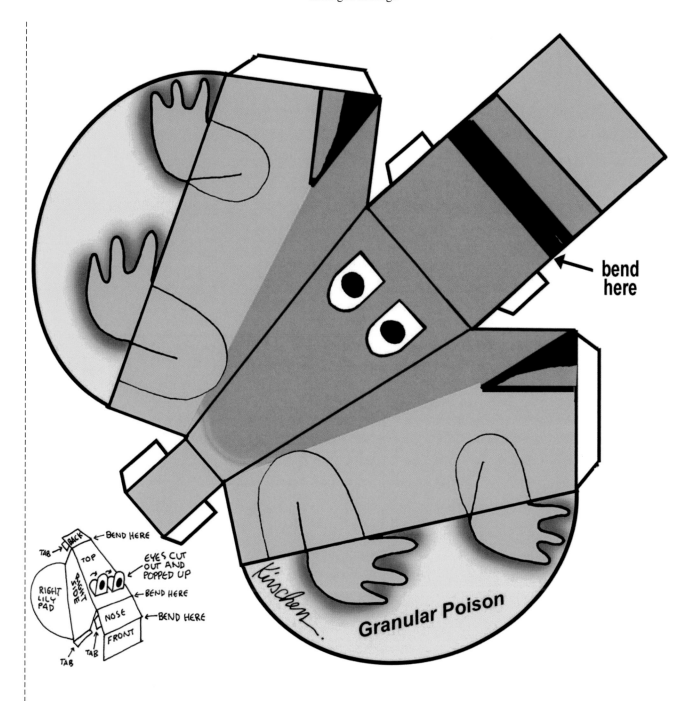

bend
here

BEND HERE
TAB →
BACK
TOP
RIGHT
LILY
PAD
LEFT SIDE
EYES CUT
OUT AND
POPPED UP
← BEND HERE
NOSE
← BEND HERE
FRONT
TAB
TAB

Kirschen

Granular Poison

Granular Poison Frog

These frogs are found in Costa Rica and Panama. Their
natural habitats are tropical humid lowland forests.

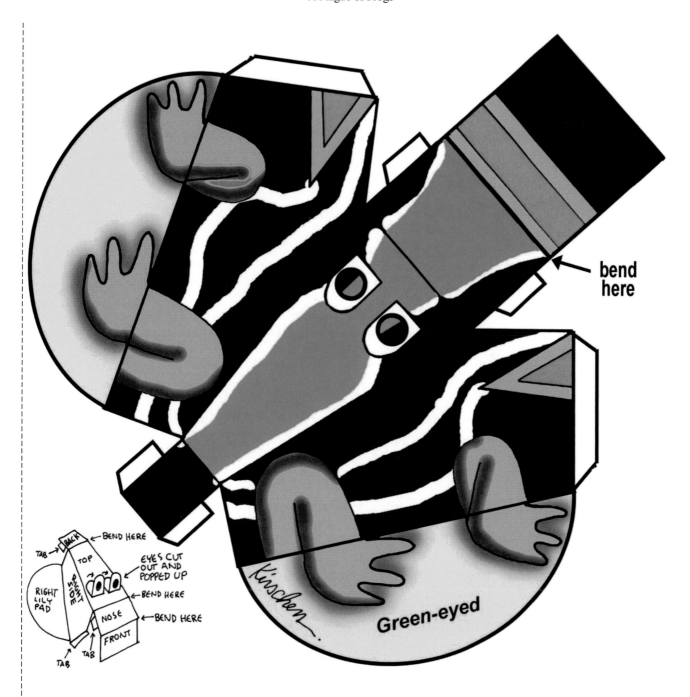

bend
here

BEND HERE

TAB

BACK

TOP

RIGHT
SIDE

EYES CUT
OUT AND
POPPED UP

BEND HERE

RIGHT
LILY
PAD

NOSE

BEND HERE

FRONT

TAB

TAB

Kinschen

Green-eyed

Green-eyed Frog

Green-eyed Tree Frogs are abundant in Australia in the
rugged wet tropics of northeast Queensland.

Yaakov Kirschen

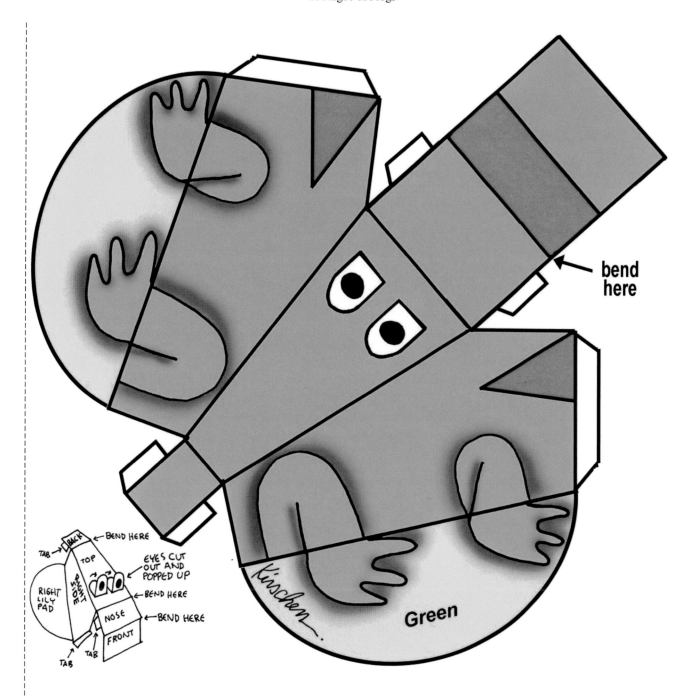

bend
here

BEND HERE

TAB

BACK

TOP

EYES CUT
OUT AND
POPPED UP

RIGHT
SIDE

RIGHT
LILY
PAD

BEND HERE

NOSE

BEND HERE

FRONT

TAB

TAB

Kirschen

Green

Green Frog

Native to the eastern half of the United States and Canada.
Green Frogs live in shallow freshwater ponds and road-side
ditches.

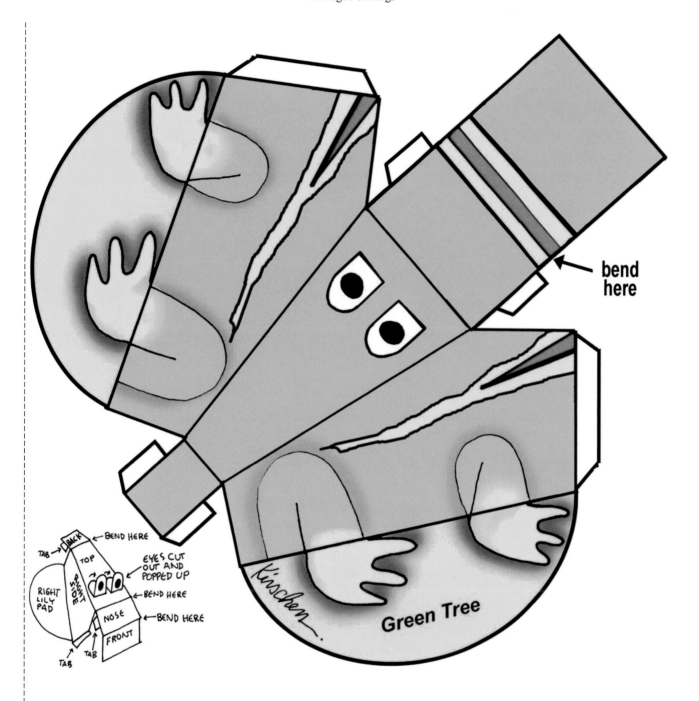

Green Tree

Green Tree Frog
Found in both America and Australia.

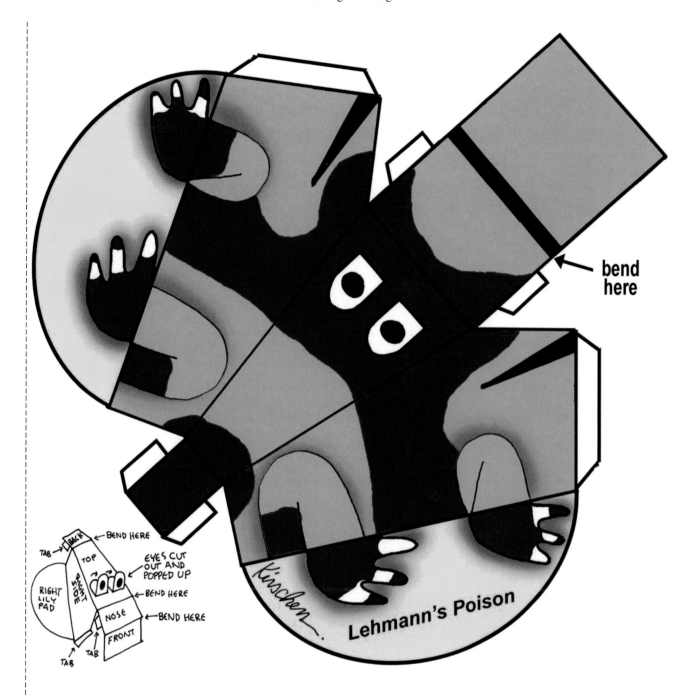

Labels on diagram: bend here

Small assembly diagram labels: BEND HERE, TAB, BACK, TOP, EYES CUT OUT AND POPPED UP, RIGHT SIDE, BEND HERE, RIGHT LILY PAD, NOSE, BEND HERE, FRONT, TAB, TAB

Kirschen

Lehmann's Poison

Lehmann's Poison Frog

They live mostly on the ground in tropical rainforests in a small part of western Colombia.

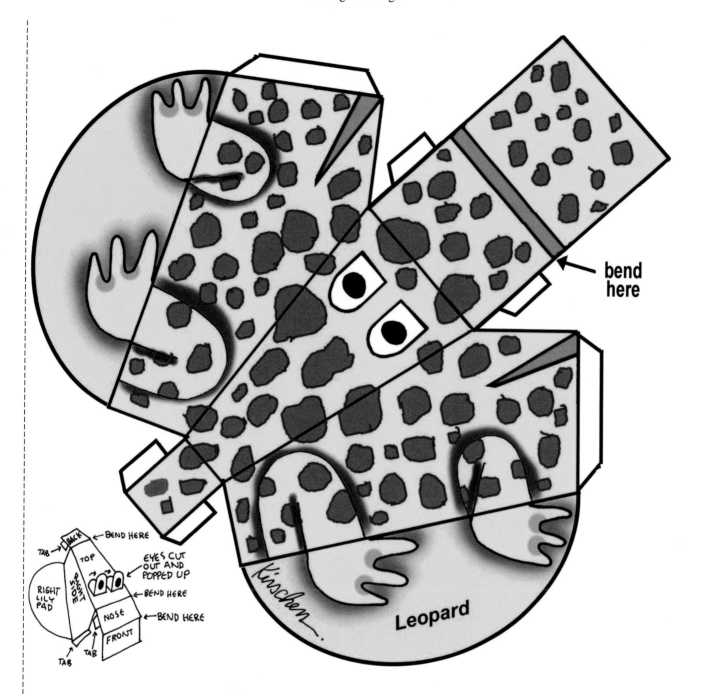

bend here

BEND HERE

TAB

BACK

TOP

RIGHT LILY PAD

BACK SIDE

EYES CUT OUT AND POPPED UP

BEND HERE

NOSE

BEND HERE

FRONT

TAB

TAB

Kirschen

Leopard

Leopard Frog

Their range is most of northern North America, except on the Pacific Coast. They generally live near ponds and marshes, but will often venture into well-covered grasslands as well, earning them their other common name, the meadow frog.

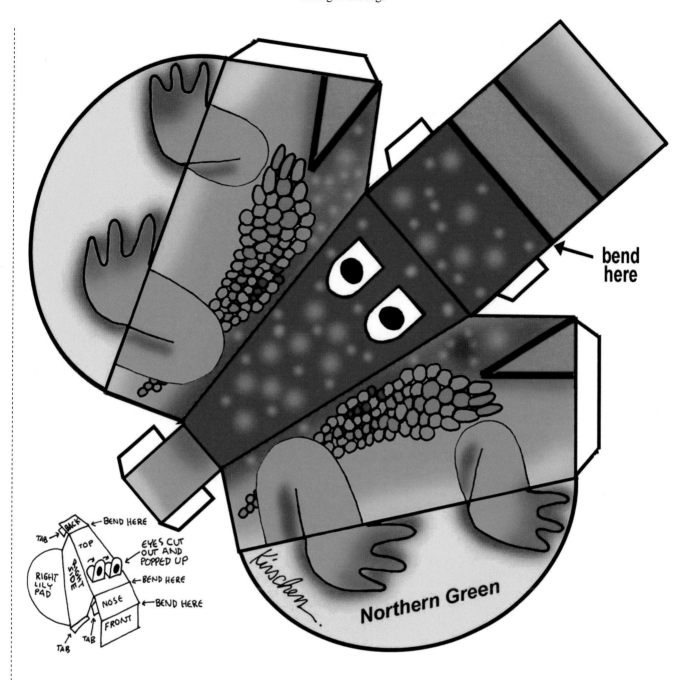

bend
here

BEND HERE

TAB
BACK

TOP

EYES CUT
OUT AND
POPPED UP

RIGHT
LILY
PAD

RIGHT
SIDE

BEND HERE

NOSE
BEND HERE

FRONT

TAB
TAB

TAB

Northern Green

Kirschen.

Northern Green Frog

The Northern Green Frog is a subspecies of the Green Frog. It is native to the northeastern North America and has been introduced to Canada (in British Columbia).

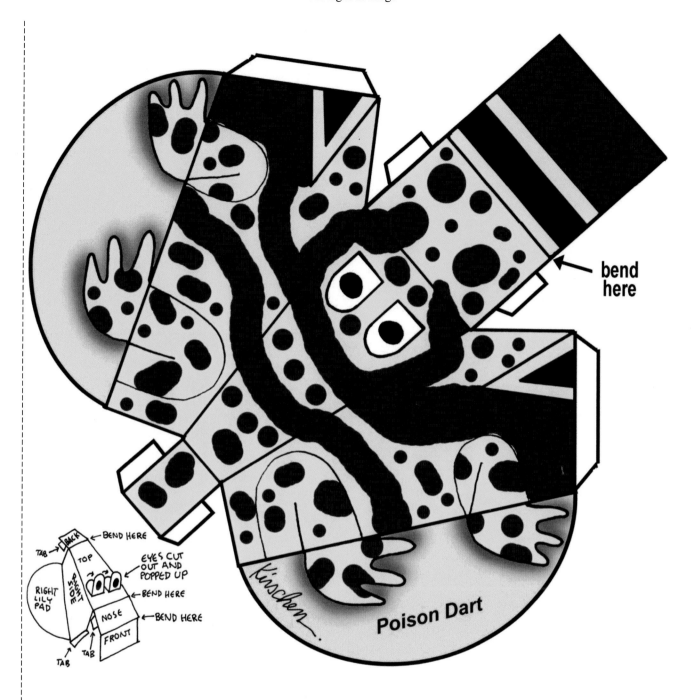

Poison Dart

Poison Dart Frog

Poison Dart frogs live in the rainforests of Central and South America.

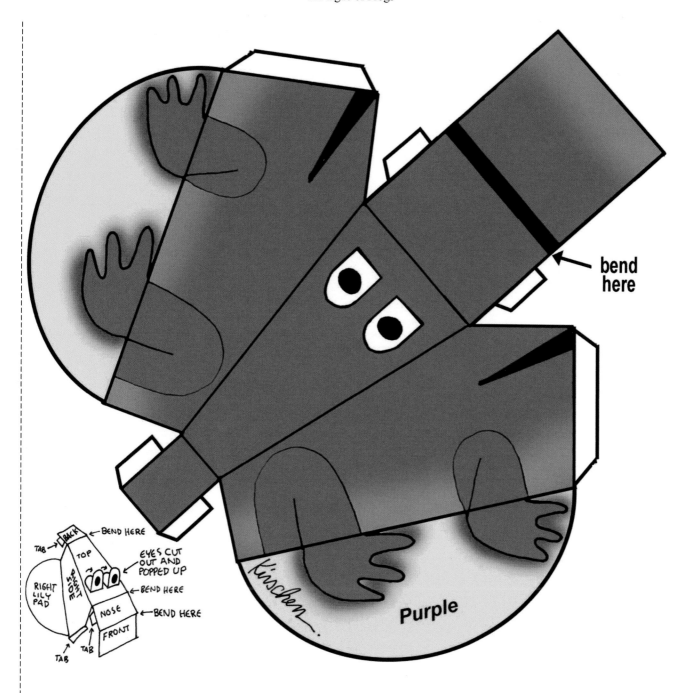

Purple Frog

These frogs live in India (in a chain of mountains running parallel to India's western coast). The species is also known as the Indian Purple Frog.

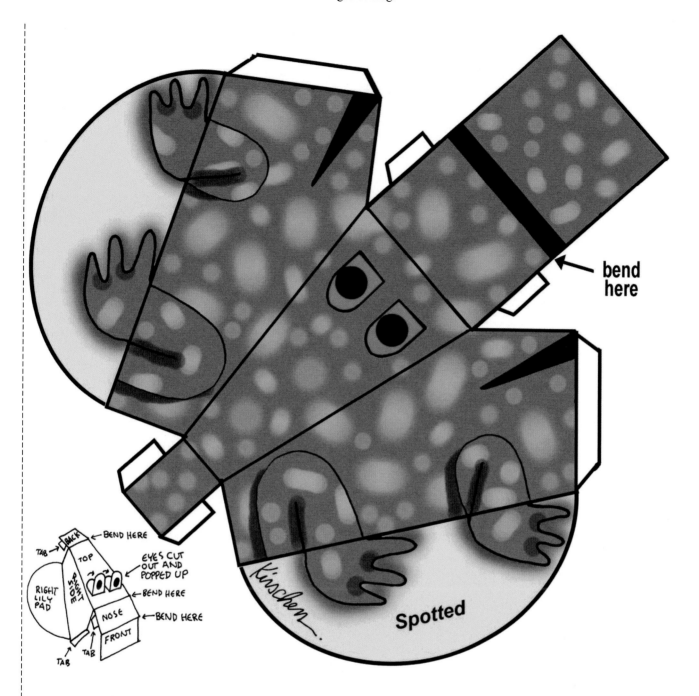

Kinschen

Spotted

Spotted Frog

Found in Canada (south-western British Columbia) and an area running south into the United States through the state of Washington and into the Klamath Valley in Oregon.

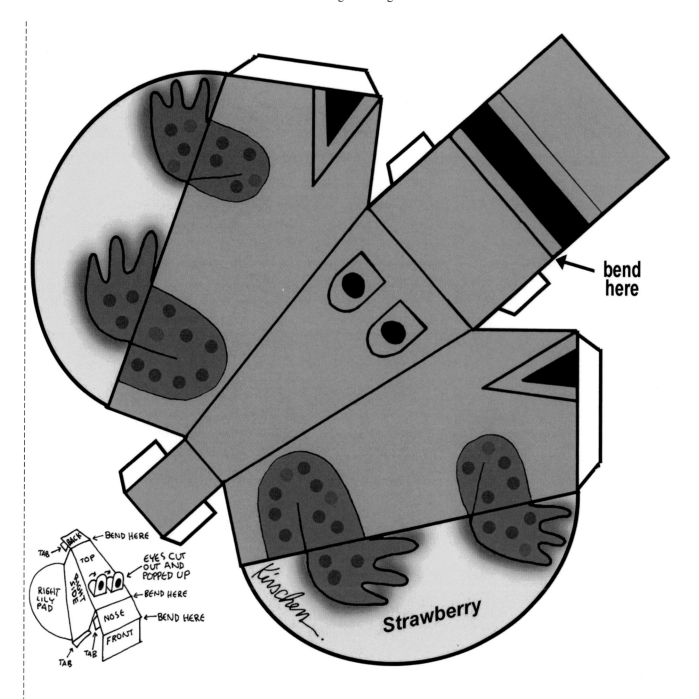

Strawberry Frog

A species of small poison dart frogs found in Central America. It is common throughout its range, which extends from eastern central Nicaragua through Costa Rica and northwestern Panama.

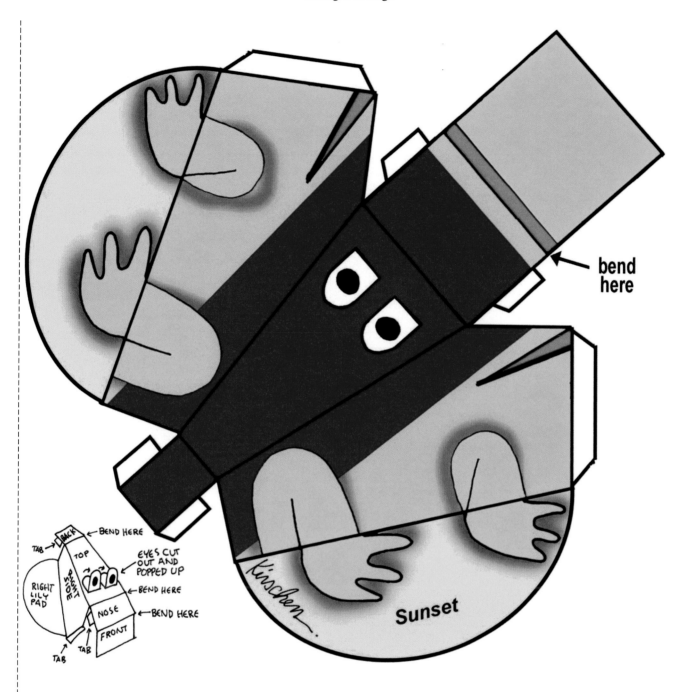

Sunset

Kirschen

BEND HERE
TAB →
BACK
TOP
RIGHT SIDE
RIGHT LILY PAD
EYES CUT OUT AND POPPED UP
← BEND HERE
NOSE
← BEND HERE
FRONT
TAB
TAB

bend here

Sunset Frog

The Sunset Frog was discovered in 1994 in peat bog swamps in the south-west of Western Australia.

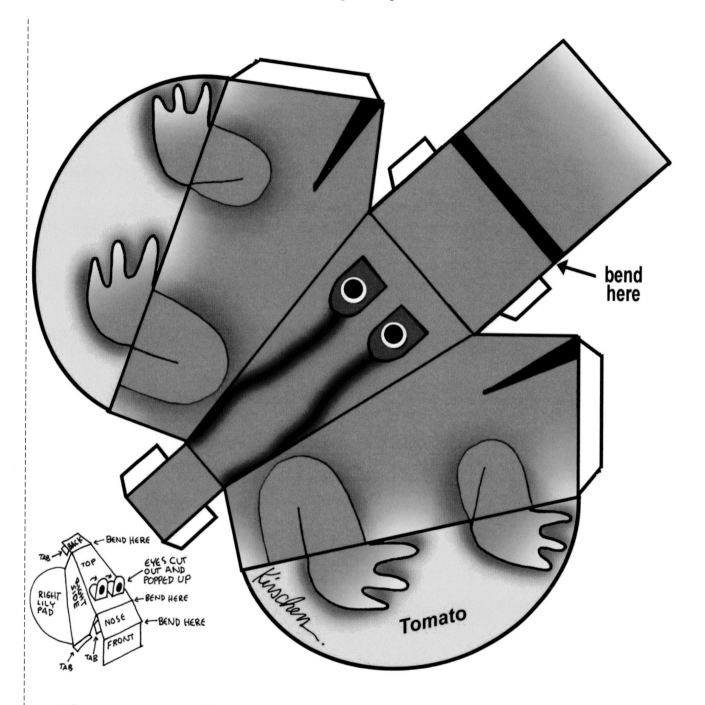

bend
here

BACK ← BEND HERE
TAB →
TOP
RIGHT
LILY
PAD
RIGHT
SIDE
EYES CUT
OUT AND
POPPED UP
← BEND HERE
NOSE ← BEND HERE
FRONT
TAB TAB
TAB

Kirschen

Tomato

Tomato Frog

The Tomato Frog is found only in Madagascar and only on the northwest part of the island. They are primarily ground-dwellers in forests.

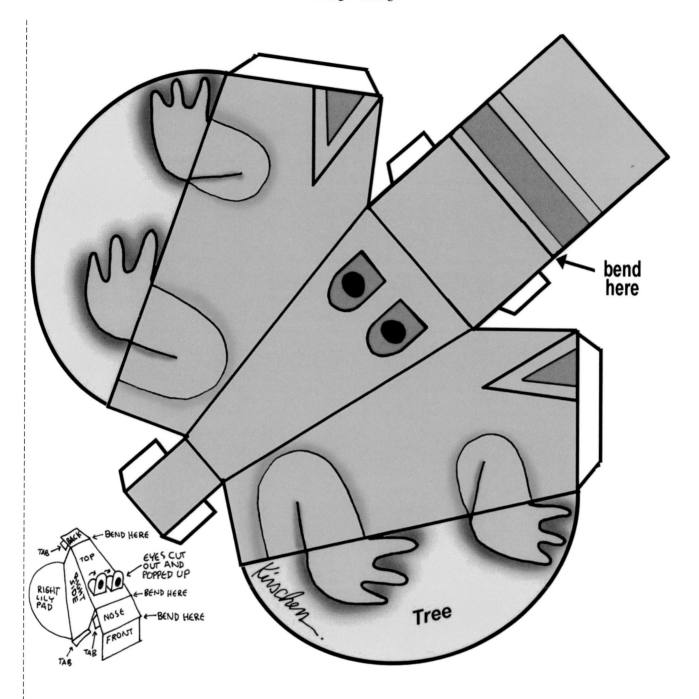

Diagram labels: BEND HERE, TAB, BACK, TOP, RIGHT LILY PAD, FRONT SIDE, EYES CUT OUT AND POPPED UP, BEND HERE, BEND HERE, NOSE, FRONT, TAB, TAB

bend here

Tree

Kirschen

Tree Frog

Tree Frogs are found on every continent except Antarctica, but they're most diverse in the New World tropics. About 30 species live in the United States, and more than 600 varieties can be found in South and Central America.

A word from Yaakov Kirschen

If you enjoyed **A Plague of Frogs** you might want to consider purchasing the Dry Bones Passover Haggadah, and other Dry Bones books now available at Amazon. Take a look at my Amazon Author Page.

If you live in the USA my page is at:
https://amazon.com/author/kirschen

If you live in Israel, the UK, or Europe save on shipping costs by looking at my books on Amazon's UK site:
https://www.amazon.co.uk/-/e/B01MU9MHV2

On the pages to follow I've included three frog models for you to color.
Have fun!
Yaakov Kirschen

3 Frogs for You to Color

Let your imagination go wild! No matter how you color it, somewhere there's a frog just like it.

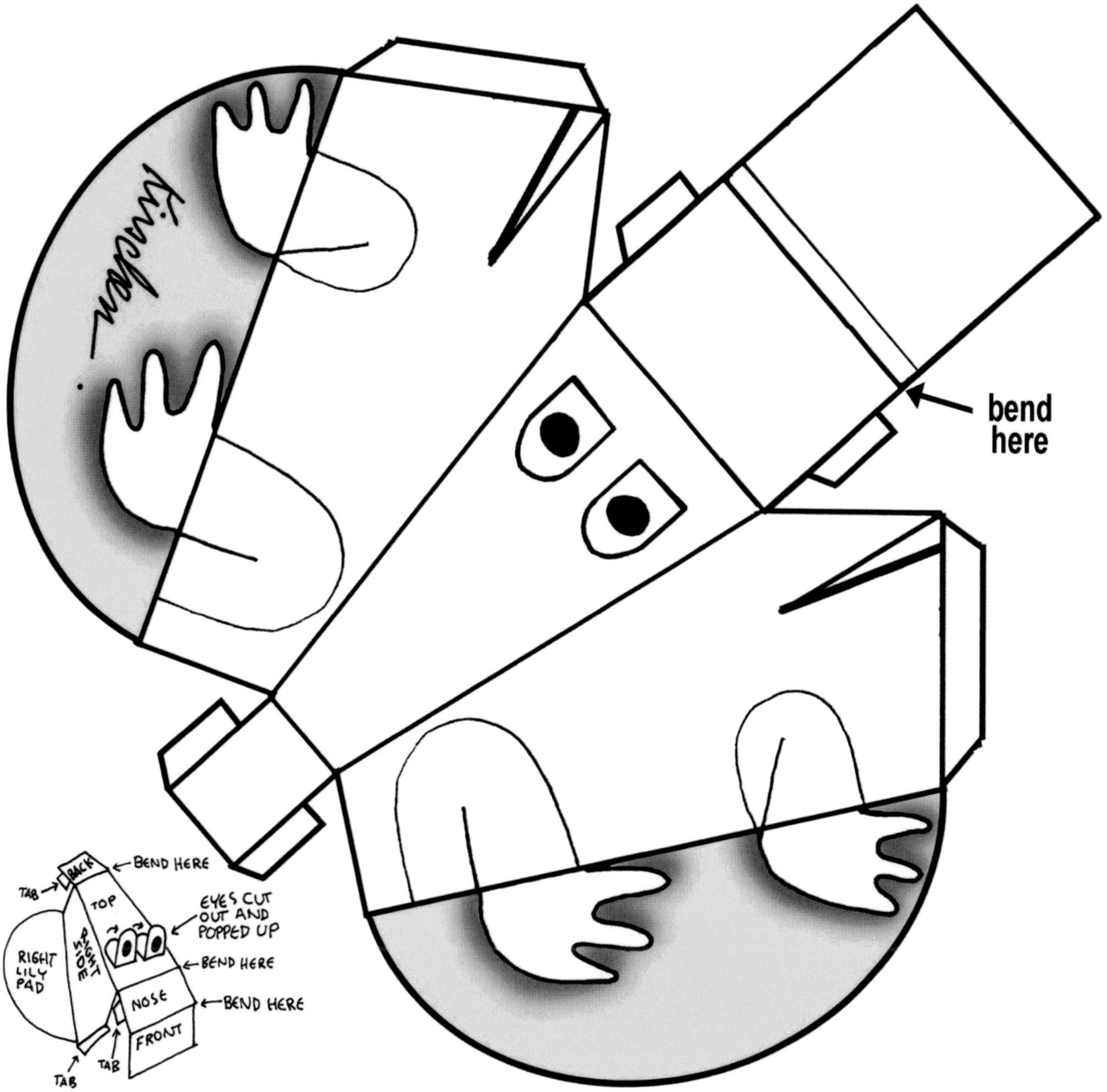
bend here
BEND HERE
BACK
TAB
TOP
RIGHT SIDE
EYES CUT OUT AND POPPED UP
BEND HERE
RIGHT LILY PAD
NOSE
BEND HERE
FRONT
TAB
TAB

Small-Mouthed Frog

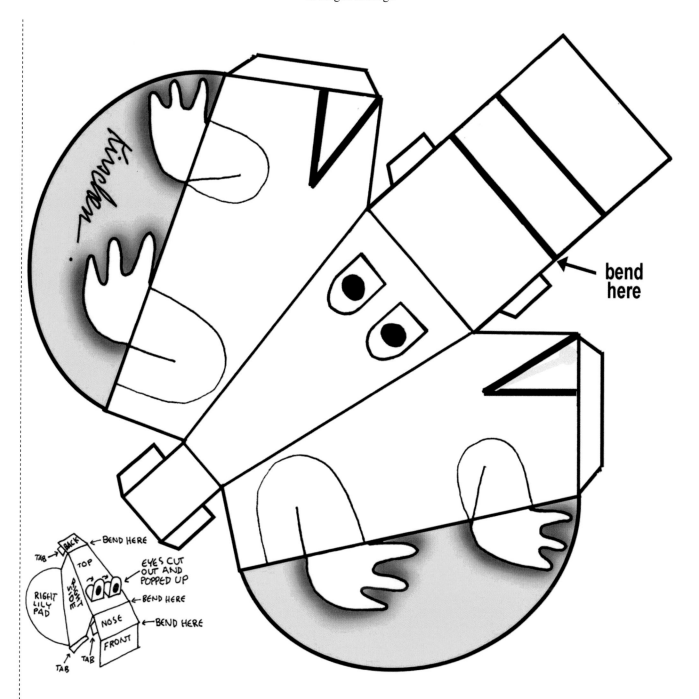

A Wide Mouthed Frog

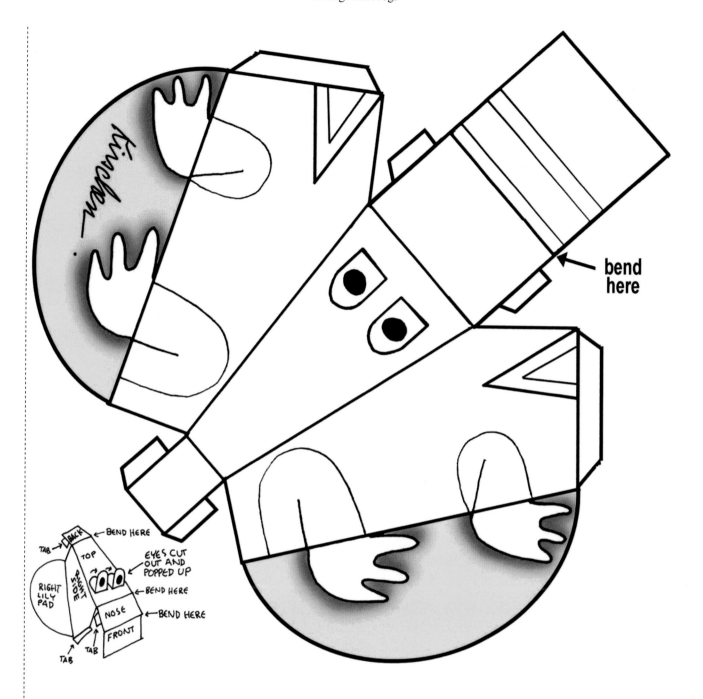

A Frog with Lips

Made in the USA
Coppell, TX
22 February 2022

73923766R10036